EBRAHIM RAISI

PMOI (MEK)

EBRAHIM RAISI

Perpetrator of mass murder, genocide and crimes against humanity

People's Mojahedin Organization of Iran

COPYRIGHT

Copyright © 2021 People's Mojahedin Organization of Iran
All rights reserved. No part of this book may be reproduced or used in any manner without proper attribution to the author.

To request permissions, contact the publisher at
https://www.mojahedin.org/contactus

First eBook edition: July 2021
ISBN: 978-1-9164101-2-1 (Paperback)
Printed by People's Mojahedin Organization of Iran (PMOI)
in the United Kingdom
www.mojahedin.org

DEDICATION

Dedicated to the over 30,000 political prisoners who said "No" to their executioners in 1988 and paid the ultimate price for freedom and human dignity

CONTENTS

Copyright
iv
Dedication
v

Preface
1

Introduction - A Criminal Against Humanity As President
3

1 — Chapter 1 - Sham Election Boycott, A Decisive "No" to Khamenei and Raisi
7

2 — Chapter 2 - Ebrahim Raisi's Record
13

3 — Chapter 3 - Raisi's Role in Massacre of Political Prisoners
19

4 — Chapter 4 - Testimony of Several Witnesses
43

5 — Chapter 5 - Raisi, Khomeini's Ambassador of Death
49

6 — Chapter 6 - Raisi's Repressive Role in Popular Uprisings and His Inhumane Rulings
55

7 — Chapter 7 - Raisi and the IRGC
59

PREFACE

In many ways, Ebrahim Raisi epitomizes the religious fascism ruling Iran; a tyrannical regime that for more than four decades has inflicted immense suffering and pain on the Iranian people, the region, and many other countries, using the two instruments of domestic repression and export of terrorism and deadly conflicts abroad.

Although the international community is familiar with the regime's 42-year-old record, the appointment of Raisi as president in June 2021 startled many inside and outside Iran who may not fully grasp the true nature of the regime.

This significant development is a function of Iran's explosive social circumstances, which are ripe for change, and represents the deadly impasse in which the theocratic regime and its Supreme Leader Ali Khamenei find themselves.

Raisi's rise to the regime's presidency is also the last nail in the coffin of the "reformist" delusion. It showed that Khamenei and other regime leaders deem that the only way to cling to power is to increase repression at home, step up the export of terrorism abroad and intensify efforts to obtain a nuclear bomb. But going down the path of increased suppression and crimes against the Iranian people will trigger a tempest of rebellion, uprisings, and revolution in Iran.

With the presidency of the "Executioner of 1988" and a major internal purge, the mullahs' regime has entered its final stage, with many seismic and rapid shifts undoubtedly on the horizon.

In the last moments that this book was being published, Khamenei also appointed the notorious hangman Gholam-Hossein Mohseni Ejei to replace Raisi as the head of the mullahs' judiciary. In this regard, Mrs. Maryam Rajavi, the President-elect of the National Council of Resistance of Iran (NCRI), said:

> *"By installing Ejei, Khamenei completed the project to consolidate his regime, putting in place a "Hezbollahi government," for which he had started preparing two years ago. By purging rival factions and taking full control of the three branches of power, Khamenei is trying in vain to delay the inevitable overthrow but will only provoke popular rage and disdain. All three heads of branches (Ebrahim Raisi, Mohammad Bagher Qalibaf, and Mohseni Ejei) must be brought to justice for genocide and crimes against humanity."*

It is hoped that the publication of this book, however quick and short, can help introduce Ebrahim Raisi and explain the significant moment that his rise to the presidency represents. In view of the criticality of the aforementioned topics, we will attempt to address related developments in later publications.

INTRODUCTION - A CRIMINAL AGAINST HUMANITY AS PRESIDENT

The appointment of Ebrahim Raisi in June 2021 as the Iranian regime's president through the elimination of rival candidates by the Guardian Council, which is controlled by Ali Khamenei, the supreme leader of the clerical dictatorship in Iran, marks a major development in the struggle of the Iranian people and resistance against the ruling religious fascism over the past four decades.

Those disqualified from the presidential race in an attempt to engineer Raisi's rise were not opponents of the regime, nor were they all from the "reformist" faction. They included people like Khamenei's own advisor Ali Larijani and current Vice President, Eshaq Jahangiri. Larijani is a Brig. Gen. of the Islamic Republic Guard Corps (IRGC), who for 12 years served as the Speaker of the regime Parliament, as well as Khamenei's special representative on many foreign issues, including a deal with China.

The sham presidential election on June 18, 2021, embarrassed all those inside and outside Iran who for decades have peddled the deceptive narrative that the Iranian regime has the capacity to reform itself, which would lead to a change in behavior. The decades-old policy of appeasement of the theocratic regime by Western countries, in pursuit of short-sighted economic interests or parochial political considerations, is now deprived of a "reformist" side in Iran, and as the Iranian people have chanted in their mass protests, "reformist, hardliner, the game is over."

Raisi, who was among the key perpetrators of the massacre of 30,000 political prisoners in the summer of 1988, does not have any academic or religious credentials, even by the low standards of the mullahs whose rule is essentially based on ignorance. In short, Raisi earned his credentials in the regime as a stone-hearted killer who rose the ranks among other ignorant thugs, generating a 40-year track record filled with execution and repression.

Raisi's planned swearing-in ceremony in mid-August coincides with the 33rd anniversary of the 1988 massacre, when the "Executioner of 1988" sent hundreds of people to the gallows every day in Evin and Gohardasht prisons alone. The Iranian people will never forget that crime against humanity and their struggle for justice and accountability will shake this mass murdering regime to its roots, spelling an ignominious end for Khamenei and Raisi.

More than ever before, the regime is facing an explosive society. Despite the pressures of the Coronavirus pandemic, Iranians from all walks of life are protesting and going on strikes daily. Because of the systematic corruption and theft by state institutions, unemployment, inflation, rampant poverty, shortages of essential goods, political and social repression, torture and executions in prisons, and gender, religious and ethnic discriminations, Iran is facing an explosive social situation with regime authorities and media warning of an impending uprising with the power to overthrow the regime.

Iran's economy is entirely bankrupt due to the rampant corruption of the ruling elite and international isolation caused by the regime's malign activities and regional aggression. Infighting within the regime is rising dramatically.

Khamenei had two options to deal with this situation. One was to continue to play the reformist card on the domestic and international levels to compensate for political, social, economic, and international crises caused by his regime and to postpone the regime's downfall. And the second was to further consolidate power in his own hands and those of regime loyalists such as Raisi, who are completely obedient to him. Khamenei hopes that Raisi will be able to intensify internal repression to curb popular uprisings and to advance his policy of exporting terrorism and fundamentalism at the regional and global levels, which will make any interaction with the international community problematic.

Despite all its risks, Khamenei chose the second path because he does not see any chance of success for the first. The regime is much weaker than to stomach another reformist spectacle. Any loosening of repression will cause millions-strong uprisings, and any retreat on terrorism and warmongering will cause more internal crises. Regime leaders have repeatedly said that they will have to fight in Tehran and Esfahan and Kermanshah if they do not take the fight to inside Iraq and Syria.

By bringing in Raisi, Khamenei has signaled that he has no solution other than to intensify domestic repression and foreign warmongering.

To silence the other factions of his regime, Khamenei helped prolong the 2021 conflict in Gaza. That conflict was played out under the auspices of the regime's Quds Force and with the participation of Hezbollah. During the 11 days of conflict, the Quds Force commander, Esmaeil Qaani, traveled to Beirut on two occasions. All of Hamas's and Hezbollah's weapons are provided at Khamenei's orders.[i] [ii]

But no amount of repressive and extremist measures can provide an escape from the deadly impasse that the regime faces. Raisi and heightened suppression and foreign adventurism as means to conceal the regime's incompetence and bankruptcy will not cure the pain of the unemployed, the deprived, the oppressed, and the starving people of Iran. The regime has already failed.

Young people, women and men who have nothing to lose but their current misery under the mullahs' regime, are joining the fight against this regime every day with a desire for freedom and flourishing of their genuine potential. Today the Iranian Resistance's foremost task is to channel and organize this vibrant energy for change and to plan for the movement's steps to overthrow the clerical regime and to establish a democratic representative government in its place.

Writing on the walls of Iran cities: "Our vote is to overthrow regime"

Every day, the authorities and state media raise alarm and warn about the increasing appeal and popularity of the main opposition, People's Mojahedin Organization of Iran, or the Mujahedin-e Khalq (PMOI/MEK), especially among the youth.

Even Mahmoud Ahmadinejad, the disgraced former president of the regime, has warned the regime that he is "seeing a flood that will sweep all of you away." Thus, he has explicitly sounded the alarm about the coming revolution.

[i] The Strategist, Australian Strategic Policy Institute, "Hamas's overall leader, Ismail Haniyeh, thanked both IRGC chief Hossein Salami and the leader of its Quds Force, Ismail Qaani, and both Haniyeh and Islamic Jihad leader Ziyad al-Nakhalah wrote letters of thanks to Iran's Supreme Leader Ayatollah Ali Khamenei."
https://www.aspistrategist.org.au/about-the-strategist/

[ii] Khamenei official website, Ziyad al-Nakhalah wrote to Khamenei: "Friends of the martyred brother (Soleimani), especially Haj Isma'il Qaani and his colleagues, were always with us in guiding and leading this battle, and truly their presence was very fruitful and blessed for us.", May 22, 2021, https://farsi.khamenei.ir/news-content?id=47876

CHAPTER 1 - SHAM ELECTION BOYCOTT, A DECISIVE "NO" TO KHAMENEI AND RAISI

The widespread and broad-based boycott of the sham presidential election on June 18, 2021, which regime officials and media inevitably acknowledged, was a resounding and unprecedented rejection of the mullahs' inhumane regime and a clear sign of the national will to end the religious fascism.

The resistance units and sympathizers of the PMOI (MEK) spread the slogan of election boycott throughout Iran and against Raisi, as the "Executioner of 1988" and the murderer of the Mojahedin, by writing thousands of slogans, pinning posters and placards in different cities, and distributing nightly newsletters and other content. Their awareness campaign proved effective in spreading the boycott movement nationally.

Based on the regime's own election statistics, the 2021 presidential election was quite different from previous rounds. After three major uprisings by the Iranian people in 2017, 2018 and 2019, which rocked the regime to its core, the absence of the overwhelming majority of the public at the ballot boxes was not something the regime could deny. Despite all the fraud and rigging, voter turnout was officially put at 48 percent, which after considering the unprecedented number of invalid protest ballots, comes to only 42 percent. According to official statistics, the vote in Tehran was less than 20 percent. Therefore, interior ministry officials admitted that 80 percent of the people in Tehran and 58 percent across the country had boycotted the sham election.

According to PMOI (MEK) reports from all over Iran and based on accounts provided by 1,200 Simaye Azadi[i] reporters from thousands of polling stations in 429 cities, the actual voter turnout was less than 10 percent.

The week after the sham election to install Ebrahim Raisi, the regime's various factions, acknowledging the widespread boycott, sounded alarm bells about the public's revulsion and disgust with the regime and all its factions.

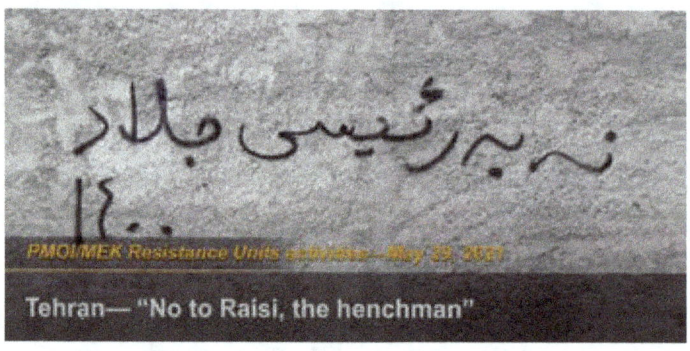

Graffiti on the walls of Tehran: "No to Raisi the Executioner"

Eslahat News posted on its Telegram account, "About 14 percent of the invalid ballots should not be included in the voter turnout. In the last 40 years, the average count of invalid ballots was about 2 percent, and if you deduct this 12 percent from the total, the turnout figure is about 43 percent and not 49 percent."[ii]

On June 23, the state-run Setareh Sobh wrote, "The official and unofficial statistics published for the city council elections show that the turnout in Tehran for the election of council members was 26 percent, of which 12 percent were invalid votes. Deducting the invalid votes from the total votes shows that the voter turnout for electing the members of the sixth council in the capital was 14 percent."

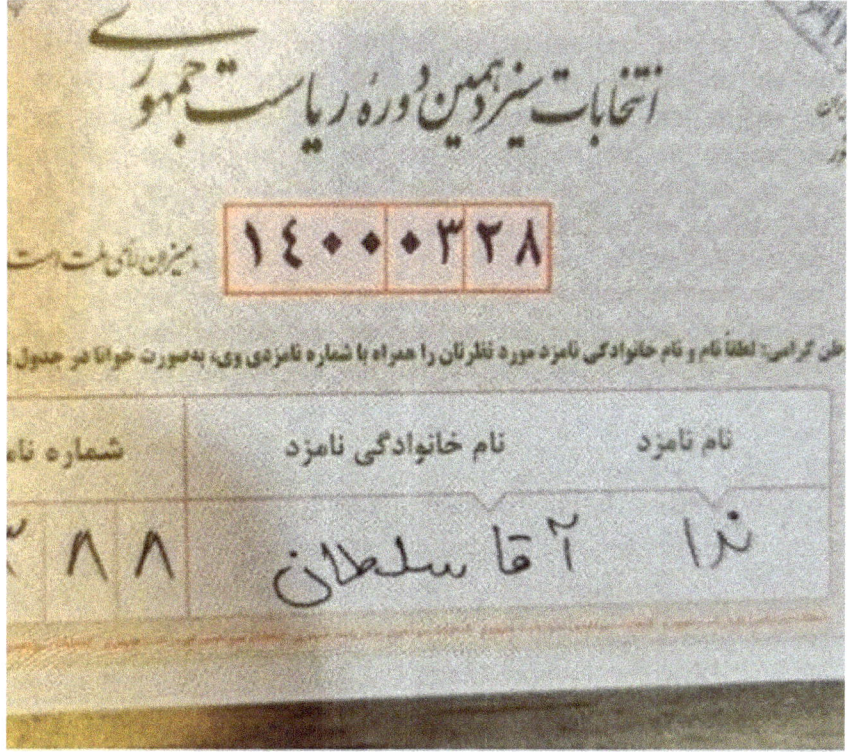

Invalid ballot: cast for Neda, a martyr of Iran uprisings

Amini, a vice president of the regime's Tehran city council, said, "The fact that in some metropolises such as Karaj, Arak, and Hamedan, the invalid ballot count takes first place in the vote count, and in Tehran, the invalid ballots are in second place, is unprecedented in the country's election history... This is a cause for alarm for the bosses." [iii]

Rasooli, a former member of the Tehran city council, told Sharq, "Based on my decades long experience in the field of domestic politics and elections, the invalid votes are protest votes to the conditions in society, and from this perspective, they do not differ from those that did not participate in the elections. Those who show up at the ballot boxes and cast invalid votes are afraid that if their identification cards are not stamped, it will negatively impact them and will have bad consequences for them." [iv]

According to the Interior Ministry, the number of votes cast in the election farce in Alborz province was 733,000, out of which 375,000 were invalid votes, which was greater than the votes for any single candidate.[v]

According to regime statistics in North Khorasan, the number of invalid votes was equal to half of the votes announced for Raisi and several times more than that of other candidates. In Kermanshah, 65 percent of votes were invalid, 38 percent in Gilan, and 25 percent in Golestan. [vi]

In an article titled "Not danger alarms, danger itself," state-run Etemad newspaper, referring to the propaganda of Khamenei loyalists to explain away the widespread election boycott, sought to blame the other faction and the Rouhani government's incompetence and wrote, "If one denies the fall in public participation and considers a 42% voter turnout in the country as acceptable, his attention should be drawn to the percentage of turnout in the capital that fell to 26% as this is an even greater sign of the grave situation."

The same article added, "Experience has shown the capital's average sentiment quickly spreads to other cities and even villages. Perhaps if the same election situation is repeated a month or year later, we will see the same voter turnout as in Tehran in the farthest regions of the country. The coronavirus issue must not be seen as much of a factor in the meaningful decline in participation because the unprecedented and alarming number of 4 million invalid votes cast shows that they went to polling booths with whatever motives they had, and coronavirus did not stop them."

The Etemad article continues, "Citizens... are not falling for any popularly deceptive slogan and know all too well that they are being treated as serfs (peasants). They sense an anti-popular spirit of aloofness and lordship in the officials. This is even more destructive and consequential than all the problems, shortages, and incompetence... Almost all the officials' children and their relatives are living up a life abroad and especially in the United States, and this is irrelative to the officials left or right tendency, and despite that, the slogan of 'death to America' does not cease to ring in the people's ears!"[vii]

The regime's Mardom Salari newspaper ran an article entitled "Hear the People's Silence" and wrote, "Islamic Republic authorities must declare a state of emergency among themselves and investigate with urgency and objectivity the reasons for the people's absence from the election. The doubling of voter apathy and the rise in invalid votes from 3 percent in the previous election to 13 percent is a loud voice that must be heard and respected; otherwise, we can await its grave consequences."[viii]

Another newspaper, Hamdeli, wrote, "Karaj's invalid vote count in the city council election and the low turnout in the presidential election is a protest vote. This vote can create an incident. A state of danger must be declared right now in the city of Karaj, a place where major social, political, cultural, and economic upheavals will happen. Raisi was the prosecutor of Karaj. The people know him as someone who cannot solve any problems. In the future, we will witness a sort of Karaj behavior, in either Karaj or Tehran or other cities."

[i] Simaye Azadi is an independent satellite television station supporting the Iranian Resistance and broadcasting into Iran.

[ii] Eslahat News Telegram account, June 20, 2021
[iii] Sharq newspaper, June 23, 2021
[iv] Sharq newspaper, June 23, 2021
[v] Hamshahri newspaper, June 20, 2021
[vi] Hamshahri newspaper, June 20, 2021
[vii] Etemad newspaper, June 22, 2021
[viii] Mardom Salari newspaper, June 21, 2021

CHAPTER 2 - EBRAHIM RAISI'S RECORD

Seyed Ebrahim Rais-al-Sadati, known as Ebrahim Raisi, was born in the city of Mashhad, Khorasan Razavi province, Iran, in 1959.

An overview of his background and involvement in the regime's suppressive machinery shows that he is a key figure with vast experience in crimes against the regime's opponents and, in particular, against the PMOI (MEK).

He was only 18 years old when the 1979 revolution took place. He was quickly assigned to various judicial positions. A look at Ebrahim Raisi's record and official positions over the past four decades reveals the truth about his character to some extent.

After finishing fifth grade in school, he went to a religious seminary as a religious student. Despite a lack of experience, at 18, after the establishment of the theocracy, he began to serve the mullahs' judiciary that was engaged in executions, killings, and suppression.

Ebrahim Raisi in an IRGC uniform after the 1979 revolution in Iran

- **1979**: Ebrahim Raisi claims to have trained under the supervision of Mohammad Hosseini Beheshti.[1] Raisi was one of 70 clerical students selected to participate in courses on governance and policy in Khomeini's new political order.
- **1980**: Raisi was deployed to Masjed-e-Soleiman, to suppress what was termed as a "Marxist insurrection and troublemaking", which meant nothing but the suppression of the people and popular forces in the town.
- **1980**: Raisi became the district attorney of the city of Karaj. After a few months, he was promoted to become the prosecutor of Karaj.
- **1982**: Raisi was appointed as the prosecutor of Hamedan while retaining his position in Karaj. He served in both positions from 1980 to 1983. In this period, mass executions of opposition forces, especially the Mojahedin-e Khalq (PMOI/MEK), were carried out. He served a pivotal role in these

two provinces to suppress people affiliated to the PMOI and other opposition movements.
- **1985**: He was appointed as deputy prosecutor-general and then prosecutor-general of Tehran. Raisi oversaw the "Grouplets[ii] Division" of Tehran's prosecutor office. The role of this division was to root out the PMOI and other opposition forces.
- **1988**: In the summer and autumn of 1988, he was a member of the Death Committee in Evin and Gohardasht prisons. In the death committee, although Morteza Eshraqi was the prosecutor and Raisi was his deputy, but according to eyewitness reports, Raisi played the prosecutor's role. Khomeini had given Raisi and Hossein Ali Nayyeri special missions to carry out suppression, executions, and killings in other provinces, including Lorestan, Kermanshah, and Semnan. Unlimited authority was given to these two individuals, and they were not obliged to obey any administrative or governmental restrictions or orders in suppressing dissent or carrying out executions.
- **1989**: After Khomeini's death, Raisi was appointed as Tehran Prosecutor by order of Mohammad Yazdi, the head of the Judiciary, and held this position for five years from 1989 to 1994.
- **1994 to 2004**: Raisi was the head of the Inspector General Organization for ten years.
- **1997**: Raisi became a member of the central council of the Society of Militant Clergy.
- **1999**: Raisi became a member of the Special Committee to Investigate the University of Tehran protests.
- **2004 to 2014**: Raisi was the first deputy of the Judiciary for ten years.
- **2006**: Became a member in the Assembly of Experts as a representative of South Khorasan Province. In 2008, he was

elected as a member of the Presidium of the Assembly of Experts.
- **2011**: He was appointed as a member of the Board of Trustees of the Executive Headquarters of the Imam's [Khomeini] Order for 10 years by Khamenei.
- **2012**: Raisi was appointed by Khamenei as the Attorney General of the Special Clerical Court, a position he still holds.
- **2014 to end of 2015**: He was appointed as the country's Attorney General.
- **2016**: After the death of the Mullah Abbas Vaez Tabasi[iii], Khamenei appointed Raisi to head the Astan Quds Razavi, a multibillion-dollar religious foundation and one of the largest economic conglomerates in Iran.
- **2017**: Raisi participated in the presidential election as a candidate of Khamenei's faction and lost to the opposing faction's candidate.
- **August 2017**: Khamenei appointed him as a member of the Expediency Council.
- **March 2019**: Khamenei appointed Ebrahim Raisi as the head of the Judiciary. Even during his candidacy for the June 2021 presidential election, he did not resign from this position.

A quick and objective glimpse at the positions and many other responsibilities that Raisi has held in the regime's suppressive judicial apparatus over the years makes it clear that Raisi has earned the full trust of Khamenei and the IRGC because of his extensive participation in crimes and killings of the PMOI (MEK), especially during the massacre of political prisoners in 1988. Raisi became Khamenei's candidate of choice for the regime's presidency at a time when Khamenei sought to rid his regime of divisions.

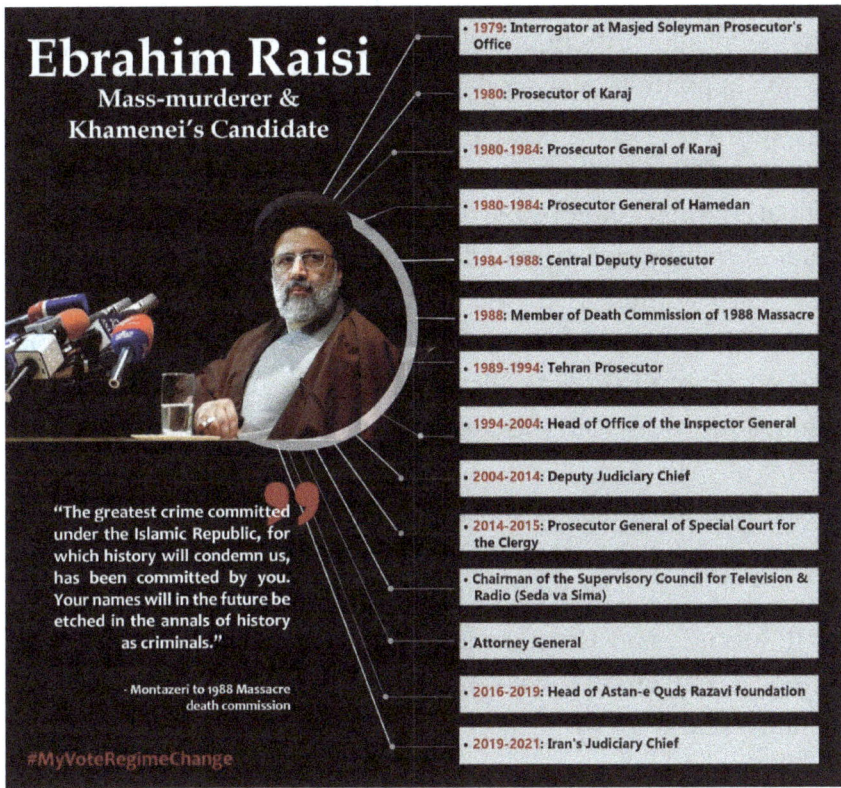

Ebrahim Raisi on Sanctions Lists

In March 2011, Ebrahim Raisi was named among 80 officials of the regime on the European Union's sanctions list for "human rights violations and accusations related to torture and killing of dissidents" in Iran. Others listed included members of the regime's police and paramilitary forces, prison officials, prosecutors, judges, and other officials.

In 2019, the U.S. Treasury Department named Ebrahim Raisi on its sanctions list as a figure close to Khomeini. Describing

Raisi's listing, the decision reads,[1] "Ebrahim Raisi: The Head of the Judiciary of the Islamic Republic and one of Ayatollah Khamenei's favorite figures. Prior to presiding over the judiciary, he was appointed by Ayatollah Khamenei to the authority of Astan Quds Razavi. Prior to that, Raisi held high positions in the judiciary for nearly three decades. Ebrahim Raisi's name is tied to human rights violations in the judiciary, particularly to his membership in the judicial board of the 1988 executions, known as the Death Commission, and with his presence in the judiciary, judicial procedures criticized by human rights activists, including callous punishments, illegal detentions, torture, and ill-treatment, continued as in the past."

[i] Voice of America website, November 4, 2019, Anniversary of the occupation of the U.S. Embassy by pro-Khomeini forces

[i] Mohammad Hosseini Beheshti was a cleric and politician who was known as the second figure in the Khomeini regime's political hierarchy after the 1979 revolution.
[ii] Grouplets is a derogatory term used by the regime to refer to opposition groups.
[iii] Abbas Vaez Tabasi was an influential cleric in the Khomeini regime who oversaw one of Iran's largest conglomerates and served on the Astan Quds Razavi board from 1979 until his death in 2016.

CHAPTER 3 - RAISI'S ROLE IN MASSACRE OF POLITICAL PRISONERS

Ebrahim Raisi was a member of the infamous Death Committee in Tehran in 1988. Along with mullah Hossein Ali Nayyeri, the Sharia judge; Morteza Eshraqi, Tehran Prosecutor; mullah Mostafa Pour-Mohammadi, Deputy Minister of Intelligence; and several other criminal mullahs such as Ali Mobasheri, Mohammad Moghesiye, Ismail Shushtari, and Ali Razini, Raisi proceeded to direct and supervise the summary executions of thousands of political prisoners, over 90% of whom were members and supporters of the PMOI (MEK) in Evin and Gohardasht prisons. The executions occurred after minutes-long "trials" and based on a direct order from Khomeini, the regime's supreme leader at the time.

Khomeini's Fatwa

Khomeini wrote in his *fatwa* (decree):

Since the traitorous hypocrites [pejorative term used by regime to describe the PMOI] have not believed in Islam at all, and everything they say is out of their wickedness and hypocrisy, and according to confessions by their leaders, they are apostates from Islam, and considering they are mohareb [warring on God] and their conventional wars in the north, west and south of the country, with the cooperation of the Ba'ath Party of Iraq and their spying for Saddam against our Muslim nation, and according to their relationship with the world arrogance [US and Western powers] and their cowardly blows from the beginning of the formation of the Islamic Republic system until now, those who in prisons across the country persist on their hypocrisy are mohareb [at war with God] and are condemned to death, and the determination of this issue also in Tehran, is with the majority vote of gentlemen Hajjol-e-Islam Nayeri, may he continue to excel, (religious judge) and Mr. Eshraghi, (Prosecutor of Tehran) and representatives from the Ministry of Intelligence, although caution is in consensus, and also in the prisons of the provincial centers of the country, it is with the majority vote of religious judge, the revolutionary prosecutor or co-prosecutor, and representative of the Ministry of Intelligence. Mercy on the moharebin [those warring on God] is naive, the firmness of Islam against the enemies of God is one of the unflinching principles of the Islamic system, I hope that with your revolutionary anger and vengefulness against the enemies of Islam, you will attract the satisfaction of Almighty Allah. The gentlemen who this determination is on their shoulders must not be tempted or doubting and must try to be (Ashda' Al al-Kuffar) [be violent towards the unbelievers]. Hesitation in the judicial issues of revolutionary Islam is ignoring the pure and holy blood of martyrs. Peace be upon you. Rouhollah al-Mousavi al-Khomeini

Khomeini's massacre fatwa

Khomeini: "Execute anyone loyal to Mojahedin, annihilate enemies of Islam immediately"

This criminal fatwa caused questions and ambiguity even for the head of Khomeini's judiciary at the time, and he penned three questions to Khomeini through Ahmad, Khomeini's son, who in a letter to his father asked, [i]

*Great Father, Excellency Imam, may your shadow be extended
After greetings, Ayatollah Moussavi Ardebili had some ambiguities about your recent decree on the hypocrites [pejorative term used by the regime to describe the PMOI], which was put into three questions by telephone:
1- Is this decree related to those who have been in prisons and have been tried and sentenced to death but have not changed their positions and still the sentence has not been carried out on them, or those who have not even been tried are also sentenced to death?
2- Are hypocrites who have been sentenced to limited time in prison and have served some of their prison time but are steadfast on their hypocrisy sentenced to death?
3- In processing the status of hypocrites, should the cases of hypocrites that are in provincial centers that have judicial independence and are not subject to the provincial capital be sent to the provincial capital or can they act independently themselves?
Your son, Ahmad*

Khomeini's answer is short and clear: execute faster and more. The text of his reply is as follows:

*In the Name of the Exalted
In all of the above cases, if anyone at any stage maintains his position on hypocrisy, the sentence is execution; annihilate the enemies of Islam immediately; regarding the [process] of handling the cases, adopt whichever way that ensures the decree is implemented faster.
Rouhollah al-Mousavi*

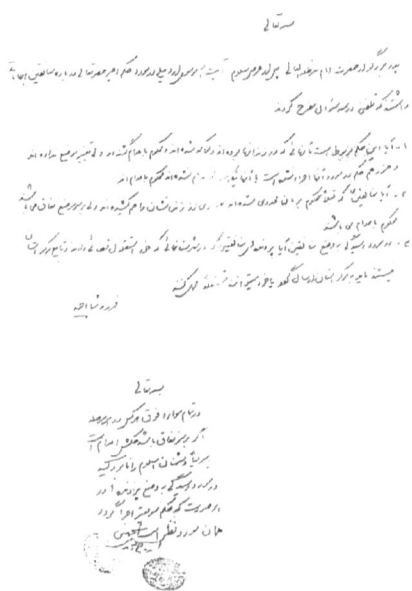

Ahmad Khomeini's letter and Khomeini's reply

This fatwa and subsequent questions and answers leave no doubt about the aim: to annihilate all those who are loyal to the People's Mojahedin Organization of Iran (PMOI/MEK), whether a responsible official or a member or a sympathizer of this organization.

Based on this fatwa, in a few weeks, 30,000 political prisoners, at least 90% of whom were members and sympathizers of the PMOI (MEK), were massacred in Tehran and many cities in Iran. This horrific criminality is a crime against humanity by any definition that took place within the framework of a far-reaching plan for the annihilation of the People's Mojahedin Organization of Iran, and its members and sympathizers, and is a clear instance of genocide.

Most of those executed had already been sentenced to prison by the judiciary of the same regime, served or finished their prison terms, but were still held in prison. Some had previously been released from prison, and after Khomeini's massacre fatwa, were arrested again and then executed.

PMOI (MEK)

In its report titled "Iran: Blood-Soaked Secrets: Why Iran's 1988 Prison Massacres Are Ongoing Crimes Against Humanity," Amnesty International wrote: *[ii]*

> *Across the country, the victims were primarily supporters of the PMOI, both men and women. In Tehran province, hundreds of men affiliated with leftist opposition groups were also executed*

In another section of the report, it states:[iii]

> *In provincial prisons outside Tehran province, with the exception of Kurdistan province, the victims were primarily members or supporters of the PMOI, both men and women. In Kurdistan and West Azerbaijan provinces, the waves of enforced disappearances and extrajudicial killings also targeted hundreds of prisoners affiliated with the Kurdish opposition groups Komala and the Kurdish Democratic Party of Iran (KDPI).*
> *According to survivors, in prisons in a few provincial cities, one or several male prisoners affiliated with leftist or other groups and, in the case of at least one prison in Esfahan, a female prisoner affiliated with a leftist group, were also executed, but these categories of prisoners were not targeted systematically for execution. Nevertheless, Amnesty International's research indicates that many of them were taken away for interrogation, either during the height of the killings between late July and early September 1988 or later in September and October, and that some were placed in prolonged solitary confinement, lasting in some cases until early 1989, and were led to believe that they too would be killed.*

During the 1988 massacre, anyone who stood by his/her affiliation to the PMOI (MEK) was sent to the gallows. According to the

Amnesty International report, some of the questions posed to the prisoners were as follows:[iv]

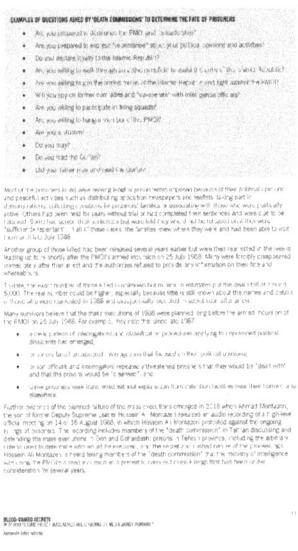

- Are you prepared to denounce the PMOI and its leadership?

- Are you willing to join the armed forces of the Islamic Republic and fight against the PMOI?

- Are you willing to hang a member of the PMOI?

- Will you spy on former comrades and "co-operate" with intelligence officials?

- Are you willing to participate in firing squads?

Montazeri's Protest and Warning to Raisi and Members of Death Committee

The magnitude of this massacre was so horrific that Hossein Ali Montazeri, Khomeini's designated successor at the time, wrote two letters to Khomeini on July 31 and August 4, 1988, reminding him of the consequences of the widespread execution of PMOI prisoners, but it had no effect. On August 15, 1988, amid the massacre, Montazeri summoned Raisi and three other members of the Death Committee to his home in Qom and warned them. The audio files of this meeting were published later in 2016.

In this meeting, Montazeri told them,

> *"In my opinion, the biggest crime of the Islamic Republic and one that history will condemn us for, has been perpetrated at your hands and history will register your names as criminals; no doubt about it."*

In the same meeting, Montazeri quoted a religious judge as saying,

> *"Someone whose brother was in prison, they finally said that his sister was also accused. They went and brought his sister. They executed him [the brother]. His sister had been there for only 2 days and was 15 years old. They said to his sister, what do you say? She said, 'Well, I liked these people.' He [the judge] said because her brother was executed, then execute her as well, and they executed her."*

In the same meeting, Montazeri wrote a letter to them in which he penned a summary of the issues raised during the meeting. This letter was addressed to all four main members of the Death Committee (Nayyeri, Eshraqi, Raisi, and Pour-Mohammadi) and was handed to them on August 15, 1988. In the letter, he states,

Montazeri's letter to the Death Committee of Tehran on August 15, 1988

This kind of massacre without trial, and moreover of prisoners, is definitely in the long term in their best interests, and the world will condemn us, and it will encourage them more to fight an armed struggle. To fight thoughts and ideas through killing is wrong...

Many of the persons who are steadfast in their views it is because of the behavior of the interrogators and prison guards that they have been made to be steadfast; otherwise, they would have been flexible...

Simply because if we free them, they will join the hypocrites [regime pejorative for PMOI members or sympathizers] again does not make the charge of mohareb [warring on God] or baqi [aggressor] against them true.

Simply having a belief does not make a person entitled to the charge of baqi, and apostasy of the leaders does not hypothetically lead to a ruling of apostasy for the sympathizers...

More than anyone else, I worry for his excellency, the Imam's reputation, and the image of the velayat faqih [position of supreme leader] and do not know in what way they have related this to him. So much have we discussed in religious jurisprudence caution in blood and property, was it all wrong?

I saw several wise and religiously observant judges who were upset and protested the way it was implemented and said there is overzealousness, and they told of many examples where an execution ruling was carried out without reason.

Finally, the People's Mojahedin are not just persons; they are a class of thought and interpretation, it is a method of logic, and one should respond to wrong logic with correct logic. It will not be resolved with killing; rather, it will multiply. May God make you successful.

The protests resulted in Khomeini to definitively decide to purge Montazeri — someone who he had invested in for 10 years as his successor — and a few months later formally and publicly removed him from office and forced him into house arrest.

Raisi's Key Role

As stated in Khomeini's fatwa, the composition of the death committee included the religious (Sharia) judge, the revolutionary prosecutor, and the representative of the Ministry of Intelligence. But for the great massacre in Tehran, even a hangman such as Morteza Eshraghi as the prosecutor did not suffice. A more ruthless and criminal mullah was required to take on the role of prosecutor, and that was none other than Ebrahim Raisi, who essentially played the role of the prosecutor during the massacre, and officially became Tehran's prosecutor the following year.

Raisi, 28 years old at the time, as one of the four members of the Death Commission, assumed a key role in the massacre of thousands of political prisoners. Some survivors of that massacre have recounted that they witnessed Raisi in the corridors and torture or interrogation rooms of the prison in casual attire, without his clerical robe, working for faster and a more thorough implementation of the executions.

During the 2017 elections, Hassan Rouhani referred to Raisi as someone who "during the past 38 years, has only known executions and prisons." [v]

Raisi has repeatedly confessed and expressed pride and boasted about his involvement in committing this great crime. He has defended the massacre and even insisted he should be praised for it. He said on December 9, 2018, "The champion of fighting hypocrisy [pejorative regime vernacular for the PMOI] in this country is Imam Khomeini. All those who have faced off against hypocrisy in this country should be encouraged."

Three days after the sham presidential election, on June 21, 2021, when asked about the massacre of political prisoners, Raisi said,

> "For those who accuse me, it should be said that today we are in a position of the accuser. As a claimant to rights of man. All the actions I have taken in my tenure have always been aimed at defending the human rights and rights of man against those who have violated human rights... If a jurist, a judge on a bench of judgment, a prosecutor, has defended rights, the rights of the people, the safety of society, he should be thanked and encouraged that he safeguarded the security of you, the people against invasions and threats. It is my honor that as a prosecutor, I will defend the rights of the people, defend the safety of the people, and defend the people wherever I am."

Amnesty International wrote about Raisi in its detailed report on the 30th anniversary of the 1988 massacre: [vi]

> Ebrahim Raisi also broke his silence and publicly defended the mass killings albeit in a coded language. In a lecture on 1 May 2018, referring to media reports about his role in the 1988 prisoners mass killings, he did not dispute his presence in the meeting with Hossein Ali Montazeri but noted that "during the period [in question], I was not the head of the court... The head of the court issues sentences whereas the prosecutor represents the people". At the same time, using the word "confrontation" in apparent reference to the mass killings, he regarded them as "one of the proud achievements of the system" and praised Khomeini as a "national hero".

The Amnesty International report also noted: [vii]

Ebrahim Raisi, who participated in the Tehran "death commission, was quoted in a state media outlet in May 2018 saying that this was analogous to the situation of "several thousand drug traffickers today whose sentences have been finalized but a decision has not yet been made to have them carried out."

Planning for 1988 Massacre Started Long Before

All available documents and evidence indicate that the mullahs' regime, particularly Khomeini, had decided from the very beginning to annihilate the PMOI as an entire organization. Montazeri told Raisi and the three other executioners at the same meeting on August 15, 1988,

> "In my opinion, this [the massacre of political prisoners] is something that the Intelligence [Ministry] had an interest in and invested in, and Mr. Ahmad himself, Mr. Khomeini's son, was saying from three or four years before, that the Mojahedin [PMOI/MEK], whether those that read their paper, those that read their magazine, those that read their statements, every one of them must be executed."[viii]

Amnesty International's report writes:[ix]

The second narrative claims that those executed were subject to fresh prosecutions in 1988 for engaging in criminal communications and co-ordination with the PMOI from inside prison in order to stir up "riots" and join the armed incursion once it had advanced and liberated the prisons. For the past three decades, articles promoting this narrative have featured heavily in Iranian state media even though it has never been explained how thousands of prisoners from across the country could have possibly communicated and coordinated from inside Iran's high-security prisons with an armed group outside the country.263 Moreover, the testimonies of survivors all confirm that these vague accusations of rebellion and secret collusion were not the focus of the interrogations they faced between July and September 1988 and no information was ever given to them that they were facing renewed prosecution and sentencing on fresh charges (see chapter 7 and annex 1).

In a 1989 report, the Special Rapporteur on extrajudicial, summary or arbitrary executions in the UN Commission on Human Rights said, "On August 14, 15 and 16, 1988, the bodies of 860 people were transferred from Evin [prison] to Behesht-e Zahra Cemetery (Annex Number3)."[x] It should be noted that the number mentioned in this report is limited to only three days and only to Behesht-e Zahra Cemetery in Tehran. It is well known that most of those executed in this period were transferred to mass graves in Khavaran cemetery and so the number reported to have been transferred to another cemetery indicated the extent of the executions.

Following Mrs. Maryam Rajavi's call in 2016 for a campaign seeking justice for the victims of the 1988 massacre of political prisoners, an extensive investigation was conducted inside Iran that led to the discovery of 59 mass graves, the identification of

87 death commissions in various cities throughout Iran, and the names of over 100 members of these death commissions. [xi]

Khamenei Fully Defended 1988 Massacre

Ali Khamenei, the regime's current supreme leader, who was president at the time of the massacre, said in a meeting at Tehran University on December 6, 1988,[xii]

> "Now as for the executed and mass executions in Iran... Radio Monafeq [PMOI's Radio] says the same thing. Have we abolished the death penalty? No! In the Islamic Republic, we have the death penalty for those who deserve to be executed... This person who inside the prison, who from inside the prison, has a connection to the movements of the hypocrites who launched an armed attack into the boundaries of the Islamic Republic, do you think they should take sweets for him? If their connection with that organization has been determined, what should be done with him? He is sentenced to execution and execute him we will. We are not joking on this issue... Those who talk against us in the world on human rights, they wish that the hypocrites and the enemies of the state and those who intend to overthrow the state, can do anything they want, and the state does not show any reaction to them... This cannot be. This is against the interests of the people, against the interests of the revolution... We will not allow this representative of human rights to come..."

On the same day, Reuters reported that Khamenei had said that when the regime executes political prisoners, it is "carrying out divine commandments... The executions may or may not solve a problem... I am not in the judiciary, but I endorse the executions and accept them."

Human Rights Organizations

Many major human rights organizations around the world, such as Amnesty International, [xiii] Human Rights Watch, [xiv] the International Federation for Human Rights, [xv] in addition to the Canadian Parliament[xvi] and international jurists, have described the massacre of political prisoners in 1988 as a major crime and an example of crimes against humanity.

On September 3, 2020, seven UN special rapporteurs wrote to the regime's leaders,[xvii]

> "We are concerned that the situation may amount to crimes against humanity. Should your Excellency's Government continue to refuse to uphold its obligations under international human rights law, we call on the international community to take action to investigate the cases, including through the establishment of an international investigation."

On May 1, 2021, 152 leading international human rights figures and former UN experts wrote,[xviii]

> "We endorse the UN experts' call on the international community to 'investigate the cases including through the establishment of an international investigation.' We appeal to the UN Human Rights Council to end the culture of impunity that exists in Iran by establishing a Commission of Inquiry into the 1988 mass extrajudicial executions and forced disappearances. We urge High Commissioner Michelle Bachelet to support the establishment of such a Commission."

Citing the UN rapporteurs' letter, they added, "There is a systemic impunity enjoyed by those who ordered and carried out the extrajudicial executions", they said, adding: "Many of the officials involved continue to hold positions of power including in key judicial, prosecutorial and government bodies. They include the current Judiciary Chief [Ebrahim Raisi] and Justice Minister [Alireza Avaei]."

According to international law experts, member states of the United Nations, especially signatories to the Treaty of Rome, are obliged to use their resources to bring Ebrahim Raisi to trial and to surrender him to justice, as one of the main perpetrators of this great crime.

Exhibition commemorating martyrs of 1988 Massacre in Washington, D.C., in front of Congress[xix]

Exhibition commemorating martyrs of 1988 Massacre in Washington, D.C., in front of the White House

Exhibition commemorating martyrs of the 1988 Massacre in Paris[xx]

Exhibition commemorating the martyrs of 1988 Massacre in Geneva – United Nations Square[xxi]

Amnesty International's report also cites some of the perpetrators of the 1988 massacre, who currently hold senior positions.[xxii]

- *Alireza Avaei, Iran's current minister of justice, was the prosecutor general of Dezful in Khuzestan province and was tasked with participating in the "death commission" in that city.*

- *Hossein Ali Nayyeri, who acted as the Shari'a judge in the Tehran "death commission", was promoted to the position of the deputy head of Iran's Supreme Court in 1989 and remained in this post until September 2013. Today, he is head of the Supreme Disciplinary Court for Judges.*

- *Ebrahim Raisi, who was the deputy prosecutor general of Tehran in 1988 and a member of the Tehran "death commission", was the prosecutor general of Tehran between 1989 and 1994, the first deputy head of the judiciary from 2004 to 2014, and the regime's prosecutor general from 2014 to 2016. He ran for presidency in 2017. In a speech on 1 May 2018, referring to media reports about his role in the 1988 mass killings, he did not dispute his presence in the meeting with Hossein Ali Montazeri, but noted that "during the period [in question], I was not the head of the court... The head of the court issues sentences whereas the prosecutor represents the people". At the same time, using the word "confrontation" in an apparent reference to the mass killings, he regarded them as "one of the proud achievements of the system" and praised Khomeini as a "national hero".*

- *Mostafa Pour-Mohammadi, who was the representative of the ministry of intelligence in the "death commission" in Tehran, was the minister of justice between 2013 and 2017. On 28 August 2016, referring to media reports about the mass prisoner killings and his involvement in them, Mostafa Pour Mohammadi said: "We are proud to have carried out God's commandment concerning the [PMOI]... I am at peace and have not lost any sleep all these years because I acted in accordance with law and Islam."*

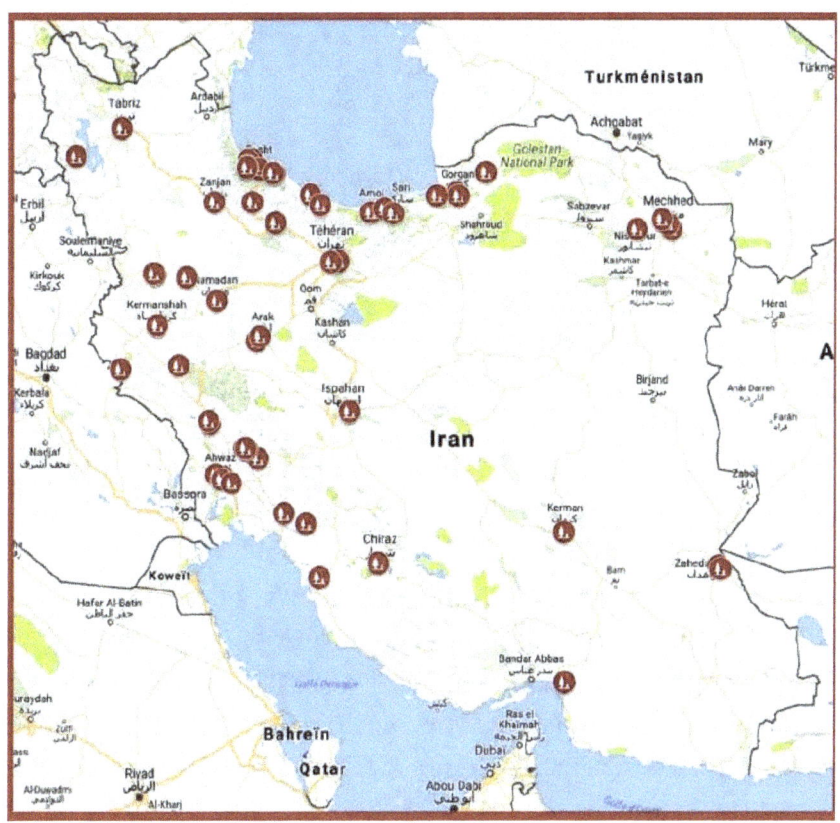

Cover of a report by JVMI on mass graves showing the location of mass graves on the Map of Iran[xxiii]

Photo of Ebrahim Raisi (left) with Ali Khamenei (right) after the 1988 massacre

[i] From the text of Ahmad Khomeini's letter to his father Ruhollah Khomeini and Khomeini's answer– August 1988

[ii] Amnesty International, "IRAN: BLOOD-SOAKED SECRETS: WHY IRAN'S 1988 PRISON MASSACRES ARE ONGOING CRIMES AGAINST HUMANITY", December 4, 2018, Index number: MDE 13/9421/2018, p 9

[iii] Amnesty International, "IRAN: BLOOD-SOAKED SECRETS: WHY IRAN'S 1988 PRISON MASSACRES ARE ONGOING CRIMES AGAINST HUMANITY", December 4, 2018, Index number: MDE 13/9421/2018, p 86

[iv] Amnesty International, "IRAN: BLOOD-SOAKED SECRETS: WHY IRAN'S 1988 PRISON MASSACRES ARE ONGOING CRIMES AGAINST HUMANITY", December 4, 2018, Index number: MDE 13/9421/2018, p 11

[v] ISNA News Agency, May 8, 2017

[vi] Amnesty International, "IRAN: BLOOD-SOAKED SECRETS: WHY IRAN'S 1988 PRISON MASSACRES ARE ONGOING CRIMES AGAINST HUMANITY", December 4, 2018, Index number: MDE

13/9421/2018, p 102 referencing Iranian Students' News Agency, "The explanations of Raisi about the events of 1980s", 1 May 2018, www.bit.ly/2JlosGN

[vii] Amnesty International, "IRAN: BLOOD-SOAKED SECRETS: WHY IRAN'S 1988 PRISON MASSACRES ARE ONGOING CRIMES AGAINST HUMANITY", December 4, 2018, Index number: MDE 13/9421/2018, p 82 referencing Iranian Students' News Agency, "The explanations of Raisi about the events of 1980s", www.bit.ly/2JlosGN, 1 May 2018.

[viii] Audio file of meeting of Hossein Ali Montazeri and members of the Tehran Death Committee, August 15, 1988,

https://www.youtube.com/watch?v=ZX40iG_SwZ4

[ix] Amnesty International, "IRAN: BLOOD-SOAKED SECRETS: WHY IRAN'S 1988 PRISON MASSACRES ARE ONGOING CRIMES AGAINST HUMANITY", December 4, 2018, Index number: MDE 13/9421/2018, p 83

[x] UN Commission on Human Rights, February 6, 1989, E/CN.4/1989/25, Summary or arbitrary executions: report / by the Special Rapporteur, S. Amos Wako, pursuant to Economic and Social Council resolution 1988/38

[xi] "Inquiry into the 1988 Mass Executions in Iran", (JVMI) (Volume 1) Paperback, April 26, 2017, by Tahar Boumedra, Azadeh Zabeti

[xii] Iranian state radio, December 6, 1988

[xiii] Amnesty International, "Fear of ill-treatment/possible prisoner of conscience", November 2, 2007, AI Index: MDE 13/128/2007

[xiv] Human Rights Watch, "Iran: des ministres-clé compromis dans des affaires de graves abus", December 14, 2005, http://www.hrw.org/fr/news/2005/12/14/iran-des-ministres-cl-compromis-dans-des-affaires-de-graves-abus

[xv] International Federation for Human Rights, Iran: 25 years after 1988 prison executions, still no justice, October 14, 2013,

available at: https://www.refworld.org/docid/526102cbb.html [accessed July 3, 2021]

[xvi] Parliament of Canada, Motion Agreed to, presented by Mr. Paul Dewar (Ottawa Centre, NDP) http://www.parl.gc.ca/HousePublications/Publication.aspx?DocId=6208877

[xvii] Letter by seven UN special rapporteurs to Iranian regime leaders, September 3, 2020, Reference AL IRN 20/2020

https://spcommreports.ohchr.org/TMResultsBase/DownLoadPublicCommunicationFile?gId=25503

[xviii] Justice for the Victims of the 1988 Massacre, Letter by 152 leading human rights figures at the international level and former UN experts, May 1, 2021,

https://iran1988.org/open-letter-to-un-seeking-commission-of-inquiry-into-irans-1988-extrajudicial-executions-of-thousands-of-political-prisoners/

[xix] Hambastegi Meli Website, September 14, 2019, Commemoration of martyrs of the 1988 massacre in front of the U.S. Congress (hambastegimeli.com)

[xx] Mojahed website, October 31, 2019, Reuters News Agency: Pictures of martyrs of the People's Mujahedeen in the 1988 massacre in Paris (mojahedin.org)

[xxi] Mojahed website, September 30, 2017, Demonstrations and exhibitions of the 1988 massacre in Geneva's Nacion Square coincide with the Human Rights Council (mojahedin.org)

[xxii] Amnesty International, "IRAN: BLOOD-SOAKED SECRETS: WHY IRAN'S 1988 PRISON MASSACRES ARE ONGOING CRIMES AGAINST HUMANITY", December 4, 2018, Index number: MDE 13/9421/2018, p 15

[xxiii] The 1988 Massacre in Iran - October 2017

CHAPTER 4 - TESTIMONY OF SEVERAL WITNESSES

Many survivors of the massacre of political prisoners have faced Ebrahim Raisi in the death committee, especially in Evin and Gohardasht prisons. According to their testimonies, his role was focused on increasing the executions of Mojahedin (MEK) prisoners. Prior to Tehran, Raisi had also been involved in the execution of MEK supporters and members and other dissidents in Karaj, Hamedan, and other cities.

Here are testimonies from just three former political prisoners about Raisi:

Excerpts of the testimony of Farideh Goodarzi[i], former political prisoner in Hamedan prison

"This show is not an election; it is a selection. Undoubtedly, the vast majority of Iranians will boycott it. I want to talk about one of the candidates whom I met and whose crimes I witnessed. I mean the head henchman, Ebrahim Raisi.

I was arrested in 1983 in the city of Hamedan in connection with supporting the Mojahedin [PMOI/MEK]. I was nine months pregnant at the time of my arrest and only had a week before giving birth. They took me to the torture chamber in that situation and tortured me by whipping me with a cable. One of the people who was present at the time was Ebrahim Raisi, whom, of course, I did not know at the time, but I heard my cellmates say that this person was the prosecutor of the Hamedan court.

I need to emphasize here that in 1982, Ebrahim Raisi, who was not more than 21 years old, and not very literate, especially in terms of religious literacy, was also the prosecutor of Karaj and Hamedan courts, where many political prisoners who were mostly supporters of the PMOI (MEK) were sentenced to death and hanged on orders signed by this individual. I will mention the names of some of these martyrs whom I knew closely:

Fakhri Gholami, Mina Abdoli, Mahnaz Sahrakar (Mahnaz was a 16 or 17-year-old girl who was raped by IRGC before her execution), Behjat Sadoughian, Ali Ataei, Ahad Raisi, Behzad Afsahi, Hashem Salehi, and many other supporters of the organization.

Another point that I must emphasize is that hanging was used in Hamedan prison, from 1982, when Raisi became the chief prosecutor because they believed that a prisoner would suffer more in this way.

Let me also explain about my child. I raised my son in solitary confinement for about six and a half months with minimum facilities and in the most difficult conditions possible, like many other children who were in solitary confinement with their mothers.

The regime executed my husband before 1988, and my brother, Parviz Goodarzi, was executed in Hamedan prison during the 1988 massacre. My mother's cries still ring in my ear. A mother who for six years kept going to Hamedan and Evin prisons to visit her son in cold and hot weather, and finally, in that blood-soaked summer, they handed over her son's bag of clothes and a tombstone. We will not rest until the day that all perpetrators of this crime against humanity are brought to trial, and I believe that day is near.

Excerpts of the testimony of Massoud Aboui[ii]

I was in Evin, Ghezelhesar, and Gohardasht prisons and in prisons in other cities from 1981 to 1989, and in fact, during the massacre of 1988 in Evin prison. I witnessed the crimes of this criminal cleric, Ebrahim Raisi. I was summoned to the death commission on August 8 [1988]. I witnessed the members of the death committee as follows:

There were two tables along the right. At the front, which was one step higher than the right, Mullah Nayyeri was seated. To his right was another cleric, most likely Mostafa Pour-Mohammadi.

On the right, several people were standing and moving about, including Mojtaba Halvaei, Seyyed Majid and other IRGC guards, and after the standing persons, there were the seated; Zamani (representative of the Ministry of Intelligence in Evin Prison), whose real name was Moussa Vaezi. Next to him sat mullah Raisi. Mullah Raisi was sitting there in a relatively long white shirt and with a relatively long black beard without a cloak and turban and was an acting deputy prosecutor in charge of the massacre. My case was handed over to Zamani, then to Raisi, and then to Eshraqi. Nayyeri started saying without knowing my case that it was clear from your mustache that you are a hypocrite [derogatory regime vernacular for PMOI]. I said I have been in solitary confinement for a long time, and my beard is long and that is because I did not have the means to shave. Pour-Mohammadi asked me a question about my background, and my answer was not favorable to him. Suddenly, he shouted in a fit of rage, "you damn hypocrite are playing with us." I was arguing with him when Raisi, along with Zamani and I think someone else from the directors of the prison, were reading my file and first said, why don't you have mercy on your father? Why don't you have mercy on your mother... As if he had made a great discovery, he suddenly stopped and told Nayyeri in a loud voice: Haj Agha, his family is also a hypocrite. With this statement, he wanted to eliminate Nayyeri's doubts if there were any in his intention to sentence me to death. Eshraqi then asked about my level of education, and since I knew that they were very sensitive about [university] students, and I guessed that he had not read my file, I said I had a [high school] diploma. The case file was handed over and reached Nayyeri. He began to read it. And suddenly he asked, what did you say about your education? Realizing that he had read the file, I said confidently, "Student." He had thought that he had found a contradiction in my statement to Eshraqi with the case file and wanted to use it but failed with this answer. The death committee did not reach a decision on my case that day (it seemed to me that they had stopped at some technicality and could not render the case quickly).

I had heard about Ebrahim Raisi here and there, as someone who was on the death committee as a deputy prosecutor. Later, in talking to my cellmates in prison, as well as seeing him on the regime's television, I became more convinced that it was him. But I came to complete certainty when, after my release from prison in 1990, I went to Evin Prison once, but again, I saw him in the same shape and image. With a white shirt and black beard and without cloak and turban...

Excerpts of the testimony of Reza Shemirani[iii]

At 2:00 PM on August 28, 1988, one of the guards came to the solitary confinement cell of the dormitory building and took me to the prosecution building of Evin Prison to meet the Death

Committee. There I saw a large number of female and male prisoners, many of whom I knew. Everyone was sitting blindfolded on the floor, and some were standing in line to go to the room where the death committee was convened. Mortazavi, then head of Evin Prison, was there in plainclothes. He seemed very active and happy, going up to the prisoners he already knew from Gohardasht Prison and vengefully mocking them.

After 2 hours, it was my turn, and when they called my name, I was taken to the death committee's room by a guard. There were four people sitting in this room. There were two tables in the room that were placed in a T-shape.

I recognized Mullah Nayyeri, who was sitting in the middle as a Sharia judge. To his right sat a man in plainclothes whom I did not know, and he was Eshraqi, the prosecutor of the Islamic Revolution at the time. To the left of Nayyeri was a man in a clerical cloak and a white turban, whom I did not know either; he was Mullah Pour-Mohammadi. There was another person sitting next to Pour-Mohammadi in plainclothes, whom I did not know at the time, but he was very active and played a very serious role in inciting Mullah Nayyeri. At that time, I thought he was one of the Ministry of Intelligence agents, but later, when I saw his photo, I realized that he was the executioner Mullah Raisi [Ebrahim Raisi].

Nayyeri asked my name and details and how many years I had been in prison and what I was charged with. I said I had been arrested for supporting the organization [PMOI/MEK]. He asked me which organization, and I said, you know the organization. At this moment, Mullah Raisi interrupted the conversation and addressed Nayyeri, and said, "Haj Agha, ask him which ward he comes from." Nayyeri asked that same question, and I said, "Evin prison," as I did not want to give him a clear answer. In fact, a year before the massacre, I was interrogated and tortured because of the organization formed in the prison ward, and Raisi knew this well, and for this reason, by asking this question, he was trying to get my death sentence from Nayyeri. Raisi, who saw that I was avoiding answering, grew angry and said to Nayyeri, "Haj Agha, this is one of the stubborn hypocrites. If you allow me, I will take him out and give him a piece of paper to write all the information about the hypocritical organization in prison." Nayyeri, who was in a hurry to issue a death sentence for the prisoners and did not have time to argue, accepted very quickly, and Raisi took me with him and placed me on the chair and facing the wall a little further from the court door and asked for a chart of the prison organization to put on paper. They had not been able to get information out of me for a year. Raisi wanted to use this opportunity and force me to cooperate. A few minutes passed. An elderly guard entered the big hall of the courthouse and said that anyone who had gone to the Imam's amnesty board should get up and come, but those who were told they would be transferred to Gohardasht prison should sit down. I took this opportunity and got up and went with a number of others toward a direction that they took us to solitary confinement in the dormitory building.

[i] Ms. Farideh Goodarzi is a torture victim of Raisi at a time when he was prosecutor of city of Hamedan. She talks about her experience 5 years before the massacre of political prisoners in 1988.

[ii] Masoud Aboui talks about a specific experience that Raisi, even two years before the massacre, had control over released prisoners.

[iii] Reza Shemirani, a resident, and citizen of Switzerland is a known and famous political prisoner who had been imprisoned for more than ten years and was in Tehran's infamous Evin prison during the massacre of political prisoners in 1988.

CHAPTER 5 - RAISI, KHOMEINI'S AMBASSADOR OF DEATH

After the 1988 massacre, Ebrahim Raisi has continually played a decisive role in suppressing the Iranian people's uprisings and issuing criminal rulings.

After the massacre of political prisoners in 1988, Ebrahim Raisi, along with Hossein-Ali Nayyeri, gained Khomeini's full confidence in perpetrating crimes and qualified as his special candidates for implementing further crimes. They became Khomeini's "Ambassadors of Death".

The following documents from volumes 17 and 21 of "*Sahifeh Noor*", a collection of speeches, edicts, and letters by Khomeini, show the role of Hossain-Ali Nayyeri and Ebrahim Raisi in implementing Khomeini's blood-soaked will.

In the name of the Exalted,

Mr. Hojjatoleslam Nayyeri – May you continue to excel

Since I have received numerous reports about the weakness of the judiciary, and the noble and committed people of Iran expect more serious treatment of various issues, you and Mr. Raisi will be given a judicial mandate to deal with reports from Semnan, Sirjan, Islamabad and Doroud cities, and regardless of the administrative maze, execute what God's command is in the mentioned cases with accuracy and speed... Peace be upon you.

Dated January 1, 1989

Rouhollah al-Mousavi al-Khomeini

Two weeks after the edict, Khomeini ordered Nayyeri and Raisi to speed up the brutal sentences.

In the name of Allah, the Merciful, the Benevolent
Since the country's top judicial authorities have no sensitivity to the above shocking issues, Mr. Nayyeri and Raisi are instructed to act in the mentioned cases, as they so distinguish, in the context of dear Islam. It is surprising that such incidents occur in the Islamic system, and the implementation of God's rulings is postponed with calmness, and other tasks are preferred to the judicial work.
January 13, 1989
Rouhollah al- Mousavi al- Khomeini

Khomeini also instructed his Supreme Judicial Council to put all that is required and necessary at the disposal of these two criminals to execute the skills they had gained in the massacre of political prisoners in other cases as well, as soon as possible! It should be noted that this edict was issued five months before Khomeini's death.

In the name of the Exalted,
Supreme Judicial Council of the Islamic Republic of Iran
In all the cases that have with great surprise remained inactive in that Council so far, and the implementation of God's rulings has been so delayed, put them at the disposal of Hojjat al-Islam gentlemen Nayyeri and Raisi, so that they can execute the ruling of God as soon as possible, and delay is not permissible. I also urge Mr. Nayyeri and Mr. Raisi to fully observe the religious Sharia aspects. Peace be upon you.
January 21, 1989
Rouhollah al- Mousavi al- Khomeini

These harsh rulings would have naturally shaken Khomeini's Judiciary and sowed doubt into those like Mousavi-Ardebili, the head of the Judiciary at the time. This caused Nayyeri and Raisi to write a question to Khomeini on January 22, 1989, about the limits of their powers to reinforce their position and to obtain a broader license to kill:

In the name of Allah, the Merciful, the Benevolent
To the presence of the Exalted Leader, Great Leader of the Revolution, and Founder of the Islamic Republic of Iran, Imam Khomeini – May your shadow be extended
With gratitude to the Eternal, that we have been subjected to the grace of the dear and honorable Imam to take a step in the implementation of divine commandments and hudud [punishments], it is requested that you convey your blessed opinion about your Excellency's order of January 21, 1989, whether it is dedicated to the implementation of divine hudud [punishments] or includes sentences issued about the qesas [retribution] of the soul [death sentences]?
January 22, 1989
Seyed Ebrahim Raisi - Hossein Ali Nayyeri

Khomeini's answer is:

In the name of the Exalted,
Mr. Hojjat al-Islam Nayyeri and Raisi
What I have instructed you to do with the cases that have remained in the Supreme Judicial Council after investigation concerns hudud and qesas while preserving sharia aspects.
January 22, 1989

These rulings and their intended purpose need no further interpretation.

Reason for Raisi's Promotion

As can be seen in Khomeini's rulings addressed to Nayyeri and Raisi, the pair, having passed the test of massacring the Mo-

PMOI (MEK)

jahedin (PMOI/MEK), became Khomeini's ambassadors of death in all cases throughout the country, unreservedly carrying out Khomeini's demands for repression and execution, without any deference to the regime's own administrative norms.

Raisi with three other members of Death Committee

As mentioned previously, during the massacre of Mojahedin-e Khalq in the summer of 1988, dozens of death committees were formed throughout Iran, the most famous and active of which in Tehran sent thousands of PMOI (MEK) affiliated prisoners to their deaths. Members of Tehran's death committee, in addition to the permanent four, included others, such as Ali Mobasheri, Esmaeil Shushtari, Ali Razini, and Mohammad Moghesiye. But among them all, it was Ebrahim Raisi who gained special status and the greatest trust of Khomeini and then Khamenei, to the point that through the years, he was handed the highest positions of government, and now the regime's presidency. These senior posts are the result of his evil determination to massacre people affiliated to the PMOI/MEK, as well as his absolute loyalty and subservience to Khamenei.

CHAPTER 6 - RAISI'S REPRESSIVE ROLE IN POPULAR UPRISINGS AND HIS INHUMANE RULINGS

Since the 1988 massacre, Ebrahim Raisi has constantly played a very active role in suppressing popular uprisings. In addition to his criminal and official position in the regime's judiciary, he has participated in various committees to suppress popular uprisings. During the 1999 uprising of Iranian university students, he was a member of the Special Committee to Investigate the Events of the University Heights in Tehran.

In September 2000, the people of Khorramabad staged mass demonstrations against the regime. During the uprising, which was met with severe repression by security forces, more than 1,500 youths and townspeople were arrested. The head of the judiciary at the time, Mahmoud Hashemi Shahroudi, sent a delegation headed by Ebrahim Raisi, who was then the head of the regime's Inspector General Organization, to Khorramabad to prosecute and punish those arrested.

His goal was to accelerate the suppression, arrest, and punishment of the protesters to contain the explosive situation. During this mission, Raisi pointed out the obvious and hidden causes of the uprising and called for dealing with the roots of the incident and preventing similar events in the future.[i]

During the 2009 uprising, Ebrahim Raisi was again actively involved as one of three members on a committee formed by Mahmood Hashemi Shahroudi, the former head of the Judiciary, to determine convictions for the detainees. After the Judiciary chief changed, two committee members also changed, but Raisi remained as a member of the new committee. Raisi raised the specter of death sentences for the 2009 detainees when in an interview with state television, he accused them of moharebeh (waging war on God) and called for their execution. He said, "If the thugs arrested based on the law are instances of corruption on earth, they will be dealt with as a lesson." [ii]

The day after the Ashura Day uprising in 2009, he said, [iii] "The crime that was carried out yesterday in particular, we think, has a special characteristic. That is the depriving of people of their security with stones and sticks and knives. Attacking mourners [regime supporters in a religious ceremony] could also be an example of moharebeh [waging war on God]. Moharebeh comes from the word harb [Arabic for war]. Al-Moharebeh is a jurisprudential term attributed to one who stands against God and His Messenger [Prophet Mohammed] and against God's will and His Messenger's will. To be at war with God and His Messenger. War against the Islamic system [the regime], which is based on religious rulings and dos and don'ts. Anyone who stands against the Islamic system... and in our terminology, draws a sword, anyone who deprives the public of security, disrupts public security, must of course have a weapon. It is with a weapon. We have it in law and in jurisprudence that a weapon is not just a sword. It is not just a firearm. No. It can be a cold weapon [i.e., knives, sticks, stones]. Sometimes it is a dagger, sometimes a knife. The jurisprudent terminology also mentions that it is sometimes wood, sometimes stone... In other words, with something like you saw on Ashura day. Some people attacked with stones, clubs, daggers, or swords... So moharebeh is used for those who deprive the public of security and intimidate people... What happened on Ashura could be instances of moharebeh and called moharebeh. However, moharebeh could be an organization sometimes. An organization becomes a warring organization like the Hypocrites [a derogatory term used by the regime for the PMOI]. In the case of the Hypocrites, anyone who helped the Hypocrite Organization in any way, under any circumstances, since this is an organized movement, it is deemed as moharebeh."

Since Khamenei appointed Raisi as the Judiciary chief in March 2019, Raisi has directed the execution of 251 people in 2019 and 267 people in 2020. Dozens more have been hanged in 2021, including several Baluchi, Kurdish, and Arab dissidents in Iran. Navid Afkari, a national wrestling champion, who had been arrested during the 2018 uprising, was among those hanged on Raisi's orders.

Inhumane Criminal Rulings

Ebrahim Raisi advocates medieval rulings such as amputation and mutilation of victims to create an atmosphere of terror and intimidation in society. As the first deputy of the judiciary in 2010, he told the regime's police chiefs, "Hand amputation sentences are one of our great honors." [iv]

In a report published on December 3, 2020, Amnesty International said that in the past 20 years (i.e., the years in which Raisi held the highest positions in the judiciary), 264 people in Iran were sentenced to hand amputations, of which 129 were recorded and approved. [v]

The report, published on the Amnesty International website on December 4, 2020, said that the sentence for amputation of another six persons in Iran was likely to be carried out soon after the report's publication. The report said Iranian authorities have openly launched a torture machine against the Iranian people to mutilate their organs and psychologically torture them, and reports have reached Amnesty International that a special, guillotine-like device was brought to Urmia prison to amputate fingers, and there is a risk of "immediate implementation" of the sentence for amputating the hands of six people accused of theft.

[i] Kayhan, September 14, 1990. Ebrahim Raisi, head of the regime's Inspector General's Organization said, "The events in Khorramabad have two clear and hidden layers, if we want the issues of Khorramabad to be examined in detail and to no longer witness such incidents, then the root of the issues should be identified and investigated and dealt with. Dealing with the root of events is what can prevent possible future incidents..."

[ii] Fars State News June 19, 2007

[iii] State Television, December 31, 2009

[iv] Aftab News, October 26, 2010, Raisi: Hand amputation sentence is one of our great honors (aftabnews.ir)

[v] Amnesty International, Iran: Authorities order guillotine machine to amputate prisoners' fingers days after flogging a labour rights activist, December 3, 2020, Index number: MDE 13/3416/2020

CHAPTER 7 - RAISI AND THE IRGC

Ebrahim Raisi has close relations with IRGC commanders. In the previous round of presidential elections in 2017, IRGC commanders visited and supported him. In this meeting, in addition to Mohammad Ali Jafari, commander-in-chief of the IRGC at the time, Maj. Gen. Qassem Soleimani, commander of the Quds Force before his elimination in January 2020, and Big. Gen. Hossein Naghdi were also present.

IRGC commanders meeting with Mullah Ebrahim Raisi in Astan Quds Razavi

In addition to his role in suppression, Raisi has a long and infamous record in plundering and looting the wealth of the Iranian people. Serving in positions such as head of Astan Quds Razavi and the Executive Headquarters of Khomeini's decree, both of which are among the largest economic institutions in the Middle East, he has had the opportunity to misappropriate public property in the service of export of terrorism, religious fanaticism, and warmongering, and in support of the IRGC. He had close ties to Qassem Soleimani, the commander of the IRGC Quds Force, and he appeared alongside Ali Khamenei at the funeral ceremony of Qassem Soleimani in 2020.

Former Quds Force Commander Qassem Soleimani and Ebrahim Raisi meeting in Astan Quds Razavi

Ebrahim Raisi (right) and Ali Khamenei (left) at the funeral for Qassem Soleimani

After his appointment to Astan Quds Razavi, which holds vast endowments throughout Iran, he funneled the wealth of the Iranian people to terrorist and murderous proxy forces affiliated to the IRGC Quds Force in Syria, Yemen, and Iraq and underwrote the killing and murder of these nations' peoples.

He has also met with Lebanese Hezbollah Secretary General Sayyed Hassan Nasrallah in Beirut[i] in his capacity of leading Astan Quds Razavi and as a member of the regime's Expediency Council.

Ebrahim Raisi (left) meeting with Hassan Nasrallah (Hezbollah) in Lebanon

On September 4, 2016, Akram al-Kaabi, the head of the terrorist group Harakat al-Nujaba in Iraq, met with Ebrahim Raisi and benefited from his support.

Akram al-Kaabi, head of the Iraqi paramilitary group "Harakat al-Nujaba", affiliated with IRGC-QF, with Ebrahim Raisi on September 4, 2016

On February 27, 2017, Ebrahim Raisi announced the building of 36 apartment units in the Baqerabad neighborhood south of Tehran for the families of the Fatemiyoun proxy force (Afghan mercenaries in the service of the Quds Force) killed in Syria and personally visited the site. Raisi launched this propaganda show after increased dissatisfaction among the families of thousands of Afghans killed in the Syrian conflict and the catastrophic situation these families face in Iran.[ii]

[i] Mehr News, January 28, 2018
[ii] Tasnim Website, February 28, 2017

www.ingramcontent.com/pod-product-compliance
Lightning Source LLC
Chambersburg PA
CBHW071542080526
44588CB00011B/1759